INUIT BELIEVE IN SPIRITS

The Religious Beliefs of the People of the Arctic Region of Alaska

3rd Grade Social Studies | Children's Geography & Cultures Books

BABY PROFESSOR
EDUCATION KIDS

First Edition, 2021

Published in the United States by Speedy Publishing LLC, 40 E Main Street, Newark, Delaware 19711 USA.

© 2021 Baby Professor Books, an imprint of Speedy Publishing LLC

Baby Professor Books are available at special discounts when purchased in bulk for industrial and sales-promotional use. For details contact our Special Sales Team at Speedy Publishing LLC, 40 E Main Street, Newark, Delaware 19711 USA. Telephone (888) 248-4521 Fax: (210) 519-4043.

10 9 8 7 6 * 5 4 3 2 1

Print Edition: 9781541978485
Digital Edition: 9781541978621
Hardcover Edition: 9781541983403

See the world in pictures. Build your knowledge in style.
www.speedypublishing.com

TABLE OF CONTENTS

Do you like to learn about people and the places in which they live? Are you interested in learning historical facts about where people came from, how they used to live and what types of things that they did? The United States of America is a large country with people from different ethnic backgrounds. One group of people who make their home in the United States is the Inuit. This book will talk about the history, culture, and religious beliefs of the Inuit people.

ONE GROUP OF PEOPLE WHO MAKE THEIR HOME IN THE UNITED STATES IS THE INUIT.

CHAPTER ONE:
WHO ARE THE INUIT?

Of every person who came to the North American continent, the Inuit are said to be the most recent group to have arrived. However, they are not limited to North America. Inuit populations can be found in other Arctic regions. These regions include Greenland and Eastern Russia.

THE INUIT ARE SAID TO BE THE MOST RECENT GROUP TO HAVE ARRIVED TO THE NORTH AMERICAN CONTINENT.

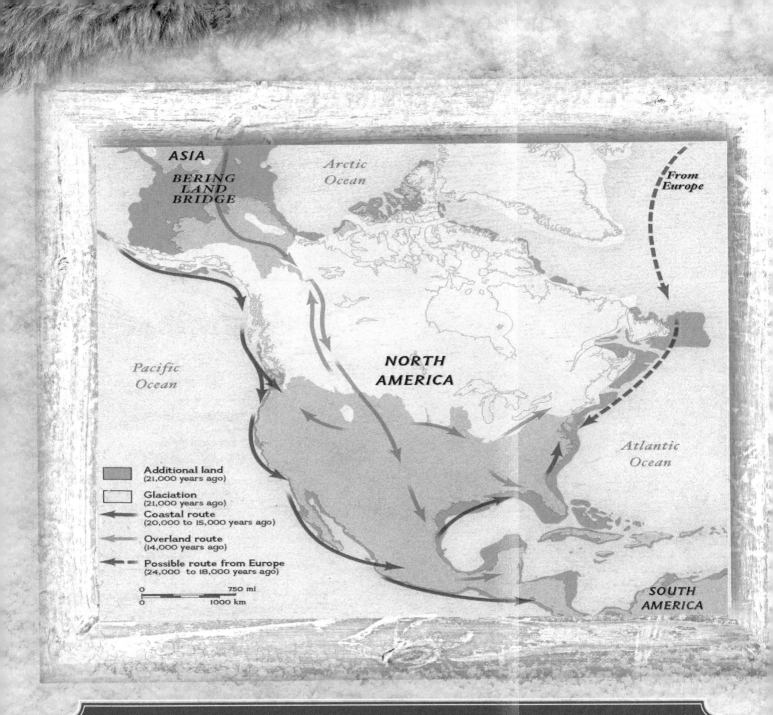

ASIA

BERING
LAND
BRIDGE

*Arctic
Ocean*

*From
Europe*

*Pacific
Ocean*

NORTH
AMERICA

*Atlantic
Ocean*

Additional land
(21,000 years ago)

Glaciation
(21,000 years ago)

Coastal route
(20,000 to 15,000 years ago)

Overland route
(14,000 years ago)

Possible route from Europe
(24,000 to 18,000 years ago)

0   750 mi

0   1000 km

SOUTH
AMERICA

THE INUIT POPULATION IS BELIEVED TO HAVE COME OVER FROM ASIA ACROSS THE BERING LAND BRIDGE.

The North American Inuit population is believed to have come over from Asia across the Bering Land Bridge, which now hardly exists, possibly as far back as 6000 B.C.

An Idea of Inuit Life:

The Arctic region is extremely harsh and cold. Very little plant life can grow there. As a result, the diet of the Inuit people was traditionally made up of largely meat. The source of this meat came from a variety of animals such as caribou, seals, fish, whales, and walruses. Sometimes the Inuit ate this meat raw.

AN INUIT WOMAN SLICES RAW SEAL LIVER, ONE OF THE INUIT TRADITIONAL FOODS.

THE INUIT WOULD TRAVEL IN KAYAKS IN SEARCH OF THEIR PREY.

The Inuit would travel in search of their prey. Over water they moved in kayaks. These boats would be covered by animal skins. When they went over land, they used dog-pulled sleds.

The Inuit people were nomadic as they roamed to search for food. During the winter months, the Inuit learned to build shelters quickly out of snow. In the summer and spring, they would make homes of sod earth or tents out of animal skin. The tents were easily carried, making it advantageous to use them when tracking herds of caribou.

DURING THE WINTER MONTHS, THE INUIT LEARNED TO BUILD SHELTERS QUICKLY OUT OF SNOW.

RUSSIA ALSO HAS NATIVE POPULATIONS CALLED THE NENETS.

The Inuit are not the only group to live in the Arctic. Russia, which is a large country, also has native populations called the Nenets, the Chukchi, the Sakha, and the Evenk. There are also the Sami who are from Lapland in northern Europe. Finally, there are the Aleuts who, like the Inuit, live in North America.

A Glimpse into Inuit History:

The Inuit would only have contact with their own members, until the Vikings came to Greenland. This happened in around 1000 A.D. Some centuries later, the Alaskan Inuit would have contact with Russian explorers. Meeting these new people would alter the way in which the Inuit lived.

AN ILLUSTRATION DEPICTING A VIKING FIGHTING WITH AN INUIT OF GREENLAND.

INUIT PEOPLE BEGAN TO ADAPT TO USING NEW ITEMS TO WHICH THEY HAD BEEN EXPOSED, SUCH AS SNOWMOBILES.

By the 19th and 20th centuries, some of the Inuit people chose to leave the Arctic to go work in the new towns and cities. Meanwhile, those who stayed behind began to adapt to using new items to which they had been exposed, such as guns and snowmobiles.

Alaska became a part of the United States in 1959. After becoming a state, people who lived in Alaska were given American Citizenship. This included the native Inuit population. Being given American citizenship brought along a challenge. The Inuit people had to figure out how to balance their loyalty to their history, traditions, and culture while being expected to navigate a life with other American people.

ALASKA'S STATEHOOD CEREMONY IN FRONT OF THE JUNEAU LIBRARY IN JUNEAU, ALASKA ON JULY 4, 1959.

THE MODERN INUIT CONTINUE TO HUNT FOR FOOD AND
MAINTAIN ASPECTS OF THEIR TRADITIONS AND LIFESTYLE.

Currently, the modern Inuit are willing to use the Internet, snowmobiles, and modern camping gear. However, they also continue to hunt for food and maintain aspects of their traditions and lifestyle.

Chapter Two:
Inuit Religious Beliefs

There are many religions around the world. Religion can be defined as believing in and worshiping a being of superhuman power. Typically, these beings would be considered God or gods. Religion is the system and rules of worship. Inuit also have their own religion and spiritual beliefs.

RELIGION CAN BE DEFINED AS BELIEVING IN AND WORSHIPING A BEING OF SUPERHUMAN POWER.

RELIGIOUS BELIEFS OFTEN HELP TO EXPLAIN THE PURPOSE OF PEOPLE, WHY THEY EXIST, WHAT THEIR PLACE IS, WHAT THEY SHOULD DO, AND WHY THINGS HAPPEN IN THE UNIVERSE.

What are Religious Beliefs?

Before going into details of religious beliefs, it is good to understand what religion is. Religion is the total of all the beliefs, rules, value systems, and sacred practices that those who are a part of a group hold to be true and necessary. Religion can be separated from religious beliefs. Religious beliefs often help to explain the purpose of people, why they exist, what their place is, what they should do, and why things happen in the Universe.

Religious belief is not the same as religious practice. The practices or religion is when you honor the beliefs and guidelines of the religion. However, it is possible to have religious beliefs, in other words, to believe in aspects of a religion, or to believe in a god or gods, but not actually attend to any of the rituals. It may also mean that a person may or may not or do not believe in every aspect of the religion.

BELIEVERS BURN INCENSE AND PRAY DURING CHINESE GHOST FESTIVAL, A CHINESE TRADITIONAL RELIGIOUS PRACTICE.

EVIDENCE OF RELIGIOUS BELIEF COMES FROM THE MARKINGS FOUND ON BURIAL ARTIFACTS.

Why People Hold Religious Beliefs:

Every human civilization discovered has been found to have some form of religion or religious belief. Often the evidence of such faith comes from the markings found on tombstones and burial artifacts. Religion, therefore, has been demonstrated to be significant for humans.

It is believed that religion offers a social glue. It provides community identity and shared experiences and understandings that can hold a group of people together. Moreover, it seems to speak to a critical human need.

RELIGION PROVIDES COMMUNITY IDENTITY AND SHARED EXPERIENCES AND UNDERSTANDINGS THAT CAN HOLD A GROUP OF PEOPLE TOGETHER.

IT IS NORMAL TO WONDER WHAT YOUR PURPOSE IS IN LIFE.

It is normal to wonder what your purpose is in life, why bad things happen, why the Universe was created and other such big questions regarding life and your place in it. Death in particular can be a driving force. Is there life after death? Do my actions on Earth truly matter?

Science is a useful field in discovering how things exist. Science studies the world around us and how this world works. Unfortunately, Science is not Philosophy. It cannot offer solutions to why the Universe was created or what gives life value, or even what is moral or ethical. These are questions that human beings have wrestled with for millennia. Religions offer different possible answers.

SCIENCE IS A USEFUL FIELD IN DISCOVERING HOW THINGS EXIST.

INTERIOR OF A COMMUNAL INUIT HOUSE IN GREENLAND,
WITH FAMILIES COOKING, SLEEPING, AND NURSING BABIES.

The Culture and Spiritual Leadership:

In Inuit society, the family is considered important. In the traditional Inuit community, each family was, on average, made up of five or six people. However, these families often lived with and hunted with many other families.

The men would be expected to handle the work that was required outdoors like hunting and fishing. Meanwhile, the women would oversee the cooking, sewing, mending, and raising of the children at home.

THE MEN WOULD BE EXPECTED TO HANDLE THE WORK THAT WAS REQUIRED OUTDOORS LIKE FISHING.

ANIMISM IS THE BELIEF THAT EVERYTHING HAS A SPIRIT AND WHEN A SPIRIT DIES, IT WILL GO TO LIVE IN THE SPIRIT WORLD.

The Inuit religion can help offer a structure around which the community of Inuit families can rally around. It is an important part of the culture. The Inuit believe in something called animism. Animism is the belief that everything, both living and non-living, has a spirit. When a spirit dies, it will go to live in the spirit world.

The Inuit religious leaders, or shamans, are the only ones who can control these spirits. The shaman is the one who communicates with the spirits through dances and charms. The shaman is believed to be able to control weather, heal the sick, and find lost animals and people. It is the responsibility of a shaman to lead the people and to help settle disputes. A shaman can be both respected and feared.

THE SHAMAN IS THE ONE WHO COMMUNICATES WITH THE SPIRITS THROUGH DANCES AND CHARMS.

Chapter Three:
Inuit Beliefs on Spirits and Worship

The Inuit believe that their luck is brought about by the influence of external forces. The Inuit believe in spirits. These spirits are not only in animals or people, but also in nature, such as the ocean or the weather. This resulted in a form of nature worship which honors things like water or fire. Since the Inuit believe that these spirits can help or hinder them, they try to behave in a way to please or appease these spirits. They believe that the spirits affect all aspects of their lives.

THE INUIT BELIEVE IN SPIRITS NOT ONLY IN ANIMALS OR PEOPLE, BUT ALSO IN NATURE.

IT WAS DECIDED THAT IF THE INUIT BEHAVE CORRECTLY, THE SPIRITS WILL OFFER THEM THEIR HELP, BUT IF NOT, THEIR BAD BEHAVIOR WILL RESULT IN CRUEL TREATMENT FROM THE SPIRITS.

Everyday Spirituality:

Since the Inuit feel that angry spirits can bring about bad luck, they developed rules of behavior. It was decided that if they behave correctly, the spirits will offer them their help. If, on the other hand, people do not behave properly, their bad behavior will result in cruel treatment from the spirits.

These rules of behavior are called taboos. A taboo is a religious or social practice which forbids a person from doing certain things or discussing certain people, places, or objects. By not engaging in taboos, the Inuit believe that the spirits will be kept happy.

A TABOO IS A RELIGIOUS OR SOCIAL PRACTICE WHICH FORBIDS A PERSON FROM DOING CERTAIN THINGS.

SINCE THE INUIT BELIEVE THAT ANIMALS HAVE SPIRITS, IT BECAME
IMPORTANT TO TREAT ANIMALS WITH DIGNITY AND RESPECT.

Since the Inuit believe that animals have spirits, it became important to treat animals with dignity and respect. Therefore, the Inuit may offer gifts of food and water to the spirits of the prey that they hunt. They believe that when an animal dies, its spirit can return to life again.

If taboos are broken, or the Inuit has done something wrong, the spirits will let them know by bringing sickness, bad weather, or difficulty hunting or gathering food. Aside from minding their behavior, the Inuit also believe that they can ward off bad luck by wearing magical charms called amulets.

A COILED LEATHER ROPE WITH AN ATTACHED IVORY AMULET IN THE FORM OF A SEAL.

THE INUIT BELIEVE THAT WHEN HUMANS DIE, THEIR SPIRIT OR SOUL WILL BE SPLIT INTO TWO.

The Spirits of the Dead:

When humans die, the Inuit believe that their spirit or soul will be split into two. One half will leave to go to a place where life is good, where it is warm, and there will be plenty of animals to hunt. The other half will be obliged to stay on Earth. This half is called the "soul of the name."

The Inuit people believe that when you name a child after someone who has passed away, that the spirit of the deceased or dead person will remain. The child with that spirit-half will also acquire some of the deceased person's skill or personality. This belief has affected Inuit culture in unique ways. The Inuit do not believe that it is appropriate to punish a child who is young. They believe that this could insult the spirit of the deceased person after whom the child was named.

THE INUIT PEOPLE BELIEVE THAT WHEN YOU NAME A CHILD AFTER SOMEONE WHO HAS PASSED AWAY, THAT THE SPIRIT OF THE DEAD PERSON WILL REMAIN.

IT WOULD BE THE RESPONSIBILITY OF THE SHAMAN TO ENFORCE
THE PRACTICING OF THE RULES TO APPEASE THE SPIRITS.

It would also be the responsibility of the shaman to enforce the following or practicing of the rules to appease the spirits. The word shamanism is technically for the religious beliefs of native populations in northern Asia and Europe. Nevertheless, it can be used for the beliefs of other native populations like the Native Americans, the Aborigines of Australia, as well as some African groups.

The Inuit are a group of people who live in different Arctic Regions. Alaska, the most northern state in the United States of America, is home to Inuit people. In Inuit culture, there is a sense of respect for people and nature. Families live together and help each other in a community. The Inuit religious belief system involves a belief in spirits. A shaman or a religious leader is the one who communicates with the spirit world. For more information about the Inuit, look for more Baby Professor books!

Visit

www.speedypublishing.com

To view and download free content
on your favorite subject and browse
our catalog of new and exciting
books for readers of all ages.